## INTRODUCTION

Thanks to Wayne Gretzky and other fine young athletes, professional ice hockey is returning to what it once was—a game based on speed and passing rather than on size and power. Wayne got his first skates before he was three and was a well-known player by the age of seven. At sixteen he was a national celebrity in Canada, and at seventeen he turned professional.

During his second and third years in the National Hockey League, Wayne Gretzky began to shatter almost every long-standing scoring record. Each year he seems to get better. It is awesome to think about how good he may become. There may come a day when the only records left for Wayne to break will be his own.

# SPORTS STAR

# Wayne Gretzky

## S. H. BURCHARD

Illustrated with photographs

Harcourt Brace Jovanovich, Publishers
San Diego   New York   London

PHOTO CREDITS
© A. Neste: cover.
*Edmonton Journal*, Brian Gavriloff: pp. 2, 35, 38, 43, 44, 50, 52, 62.
United Press International: pp. 6, 8, 9, 11, 33, 47, 59.
Copyright *The Globe and Mail:* pp. 14, 23.
Howard Livick: pp. 18, 21.
Photo courtesy of *Sault Daily Star:* pp. 24, 26, 29.
*The Indianapolis News,* Bob Doeppers: p. 30.
*Edmonton Journal*, Steve Makris: pp. 37, 40.
*Edmonton Journal*, Bruce Edwards: p. 49.
*Edmonton Journal*, Dean Bicknell: p. 57.

Copyright © 1982 by Sue Burchard
All rights reserved. No part of this publication may be reproduced or transmitted in any form or by any means, electronic or mechanical, including photocopy, recording, or any information storage and retrieval system, without permission in writing from the publisher.

Requests for permission to make copies of any part of the work should be mailed to: Permissions, Harcourt Brace Jovanovich, Publishers, 757 Third Avenue, New York, N.Y. 10017.

Printed in the United States of America

LIBRARY OF CONGRESS CATALOGING IN PUBLICATION DATA
Burchard, S. H.   Wayne Gretzky. (Sports star)
SUMMARY: A biography for beginning readers of the star player of Canada's Edmonton Oilers hockey team who has broken many NHL scoring records.
1. Gretzky, Wayne, 1961-   —Juvenile literature.
2. Hockey players—Canada—Biography—Juvenile literature.
3. National Hockey League—Juvenile literature.
[1. Gretzky, Wayne, 1961-   . 2. Hockey players]
I. Title.  II. Series.
GV848.5.G73B87   1982    796.96'2'0924 [B] [92]    82-47931
ISBN 0-15-278046-7                ISBN 0-15-278047-5 (pbk.)

B C D E            First edition            B C D E (pbk.)

# CONTENTS

| | | | |
|---|---|---|---|
| 1 | ★ | The Great Gretzky | 7 |
| 2 | ★ | Growing Up Playing Hockey | 15 |
| 3 | ★ | The Young Professional | 27 |
| 4 | ★ | A Team Grows Up | 41 |
| 5 | ★ | The 1981–82 Season | 53 |
| | | Playing Record | 64 |

★ SPORTS STAR ★ WAYNE GRETZKY

# 1

# THE GREAT GRETZKY

With six minutes left in a game against the Buffalo Sabres, Wayne Gretzky of the Edmonton Oilers scooped up a loose puck, zigged and zagged his way through two defenders, and finally broke loose. He skated in alone toward the Buffalo goal and from ten feet out fired a shot through the legs of Don Edwards, the Buffalo goaltender. The goal put the Oilers ahead by a score of 4-3.

Wayne is hugged by teammates after scoring his record goal.

★ SPORTS STAR ★ WAYNE GRETZKY ★

Oiler Wayne Gretzky shoots the puck past goalie Don Edwards to score his record-breaking seventy-seventh goal.

The date was February 24, 1982. It was an important moment in hockey history. With this goal, his seventy-seventh, twenty-one-year-old Wayne Gretzky had just broken Phil Esposito's record for the most goals ever scored in one season.

The sellout crowd of over 17,000 hockey fans stood and cheered. His teammates almost mobbed him in their excitement and enthusiasm. Phil Esposito, who was watching from the stands, came down to the ice to offer his own congratulations and to formally present Wayne Gretzky with the history-making puck. As Esposito gave the young hockey super hero a bear hug, Wayne told him, "It's a tremendous relief."

Wayne Gretzky gets a pat on the back from former record-holder Phil Esposito.

# SPORTS STAR ★ WAYNE GRETZKY

Wayne was used to being the center of attention, but as he got nearer and nearer to breaking the record, the press and his fans almost never left him alone. It was a relief to break the record and get back to the business of concentrating primarily on winning games for the Oilers. While it was fun to be hailed as the greatest hockey player today, Wayne's main interest was in helping the Oilers to a championship year and maybe even to winning the Stanley Cup.

After the applause died down and the award ceremony was over, the young Oiler team skated back onto the ice for the final minutes of the game. With about a minute and a half to go, Wayne slapped in a shot from the right slot for goal number 78. Then with seventeen seconds remaining, Gretzky

A smiling Wayne Gretzky skates off the ice with the history-making puck.

# SPORTS STAR ★ WAYNE GRETZKY

completed an amazing three-goal, five-point night with a shot from the top of the left circle.

Wayne was having quite a year, and it wasn't over yet. In his third season in the National Hockey League, it seemed very likely that the curly-haired, blond young man who was about five feet, eleven inches tall, who weighed barely 165 pounds, and who was just twenty-one years old would break all the major NHL single-season scoring records.

Wayne Gretzky does not look like one of the best hockey players of all time. His skating style, with his elbows flying out behind him, makes him look like a scared chicken trying to escape from a fox. But there is no doubt that he will be one of the all-time great hockey players.

His 1981-82 season will go down in the record books as the best so far for any player in the long history of professional hockey. The fans call him The Great Gretzky. It is a nickname that Wayne worked hard to earn. In fact, he has been working at being a great hockey player since he was two years old.

SPORTS STAR  WAYNE GRETZKY

# 2
# GROWING UP PLAYING HOCKEY

Walter and Phyllis Gretzky raised their large family in the town of Brantford, Ontario, Canada. Walter worked for the Bell Telephone Company, but he had always wanted to be a hockey player. He once played on Junior B teams, but he was told that he was too small to make it to the pros. He wanted his own children to have every chance to play the game he loved.

Ten-year-old Wayne Gretzky

# SPORTS STAR ★ WAYNE GRETZKY

The first of the Gretzky children, Wayne Douglas, was born on January 26, 1961. Later a daughter and three more sons were added to the family.

Even before his father got him his first pair of skates, Wayne Gretzky seemed drawn to hockey. On Saturday nights his parents frequently took their two-year-old son to visit his grandmother, Mrs. Mary Gretzky. She was a big hockey fan and always watched Hockey Night on Canadian television while she took care of her grandson.

Young Wayne tried to copy the moves of the players by sliding around in his stocking feet on the well-polished pine living-room floor. His grandmother bought him a little souvenir hockey stick and small ball. She would sit in her big chair and be Wayne's goaltender. By the end of an evening of baby-sitting, Mrs. Gretzky often had bruises on her legs from getting hit with the souvenir hockey stick.

Wayne got his first skates before he was three years old. They had single blades. When his father could not find a stick small enough for Wayne, he bought the lightest one he could find and carefully shaved it down to the right size.

Walter Gretzky built an ice rink in the backyard. He did not flood it with a hose because it might have been too lumpy. Instead, once the ground was frozen and the grass cut very short, he got out his lawn sprinkler and laid on coat after coat. Every night during the winter months, when he got home from his job, he turned on the sprinkler and added another smooth coat.

# SPORTS STAR       WAYNE GRETZKY

One year the sprinkler broke. Mr. Gretzky sent his wife to buy a new one. The clerks in the store thought she was a little crazy buying a lawn sprinkler in the middle of February.

Walter Gretzky was an amazing teacher, and he demanded a lot from his star pupil. He put some tin cans on the ice and made Wayne skate around and between them. In addition, Wayne had to jump over sticks as his father sent him passes. Mr. Gretzky placed all kinds of targets on the goal net, and Wayne would spend hours shooting at them. After supper he would go out to practice until bedtime with the aid of lights his father had strung up around the rink.

All of the Gretzky children turned out to be fine athletes. Wayne's sister became a national track star, and his brothers all eventually played hockey. Wayne, though, did not grow up playing hockey with them because they were much younger. There was a six-year difference in age between Wayne and Keith, the second Gretzky son.

Wayne, however, often had company on the ice. Walter Gretzky's ice rink was a big attraction in the neighborhood. It was almost always filled with kids who came to skate or just to watch.

Walter Gretzky shovels snow
from his backyard hockey rink.

# SPORTS STAR    WAYNE GRETZKY

From a very early age, however, Wayne took the game much more seriously than most of his friends. The usual boyhood toys and games did not interest him much. He worked hour after hour to perform perfectly every move and play his father taught him.

When Wayne was five, Walter Gretzky drove him all over the Brantford area to find an organized team that would take his son. He was not successful. No one would let Wayne play until he was six.

In the meantime, Mr. Gretzky continued to teach him. When Wayne finally got on a team as a six-year-old, his father took over as the coach. One drill helped Wayne tremendously—perhaps more than it did any of the other players. Walter Gretzky shot the puck down the boards toward a corner, where it would bounce off and roll

Wayne's school

behind the net. He told the boys to chase it. Then he made the same shot again. This time Coach Gretzky himself cut across to where it was rolling. He told his team they must not just follow the puck. They had to know where it was going to go. In the years to come, Wayne would show an uncanny ability to always know where the puck would end up after it was hit.

In his first year of organized play, six-year-old Wayne scored only one goal, but he was playing with mostly ten-year-olds. He got 27 goals the next year and 104 goals the year after that.

SPORTS STAR  WAYNE GRETZKY

Wayne had his most sensational year as a novice when he was ten years old. He scored 378 goals in 68 games. He was a four-foot-four, seventy-pound dynamo. The Brantford area hockey fans stood in long lines to get into the arena to watch the wonder kid of hockey play. Wayne was often interviewed on national television and written about in many newspapers and magazines. He got used to being famous at a young age.

In 1975, when Wayne was fourteen, the Gretzky family made a tough decision. His parents were worried that all the excitement Wayne was causing in Brantford made it difficult for him to have a normal childhood. In addition, there were parents of Wayne's teammates who resented the attention Wayne was getting. He was also running out of competition.

In Toronto there was an organization of hockey players under twenty years of age called the Young Nats. Toronto was also the closest large city to Brantford. In a place as large as Toronto, Wayne would not always be the center of attention, and he could meet players closer to his own ability.

The decision was made for Wayne to move to Toronto. The Gretzkys, at various tournaments, had met another hockey family, the Cornishes, who lived near Toronto. Wayne went to live with them. They also had a son playing for the Young Nats.

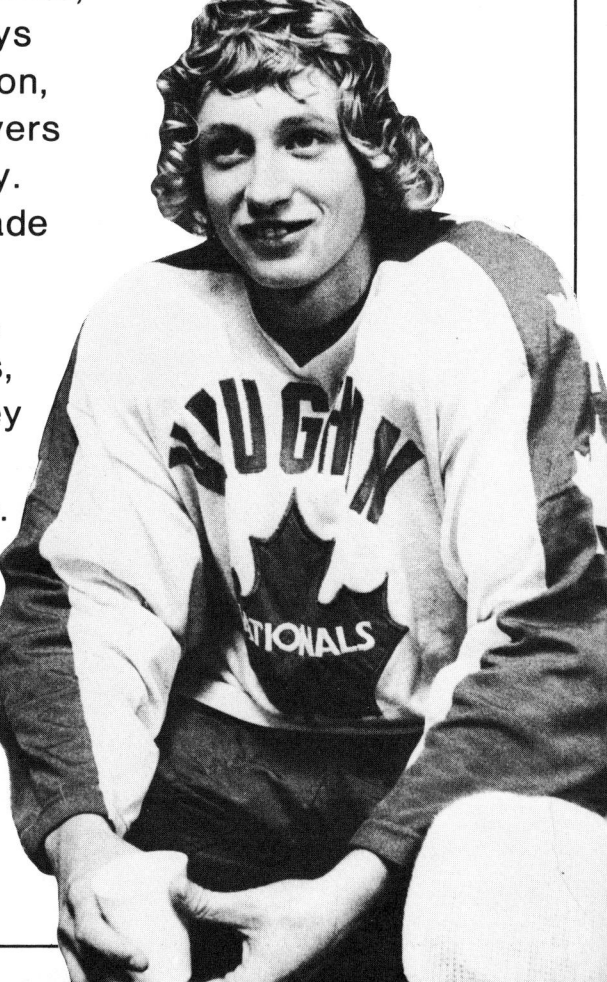

SPORTS STAR  WAYNE GRETZKY

Wayne joined the team and attended high school there.

In his first game for the Nats Junior B team, Wayne scored two goals. He went on to win the league's rookie-of-the-year award.

After playing for two years for the Young Nats, Wayne was drafted by the Sault Ste. Marie Greyhounds. He was sixteen years old. In his first game for the Greyhounds, he scored three goals. He ended the season

Wayne holding the puck he used to tie the goal-scoring record (67) for a rookie in Junior A play

with 70 goals and 112 assists. He won trophies as the league's best rookie and most gentlemanly player.

Wayne lived with Jim and Sylvia Bodner, friends of his parents who had moved from Brantford to Sault Ste. Marie. Wayne called home often. His only problem was that he had trouble keeping up with his grade eleven school work. Hockey demanded too much of his time.

The fans fell in love with Wayne. Unlike many hockey players, he was polite, well spoken, and charming. Even though the team was not very good, the Greyhounds set attendance records wherever they played. People came to see the dazzling sixteen-year-old playing with twenty-year-olds.

 SPORTS STAR  WAYNE GRETZKY

# 3

# THE YOUNG PROFESSIONAL

In one year of playing Junior A hockey in Sault Ste. Marie, Wayne had attracted much national attention. Pro scouts attended almost every game. After the season was over, there was a great deal of guessing about whether or not Wayne Gretzky would be back for another year.

There were some scouts, however, who felt quite sure that Wayne Gretzky would never make it as a professional hockey

Wayne in action for the
Sault Ste. Marie Greyhounds

SPORTS STAR  WAYNE GRETZKY

player. He was much too scrawny. At seventeen he weighed only 161 pounds. His face was so narrow that his helmet looked about two sizes too big for him. He was not an especially good skater, and his shot was not too strong.

On the other hand, there were other scouts who believed that Wayne Gretzky was the best junior player they had ever seen. He made excellent use of the space behind the net. Wayne would skate in back of the net, where for a few seconds he was safe from attackers, duck down, and feed passes to his teammates. If no one came after him, Wayne darted in front of the goal himself.

He displayed an incredible ability to stick-handle. He perfected his technique by long hours of practice during the summer,

Gretzky with Greyhounds line-mates Dan Lucas and Paul Mancini

stick-handling tennis balls in the driveway of his parents' home. Tennis balls are harder to hit than pucks. (The neighbors complained of broken windows on several occasions.)

Wayne could also pick pucks out of the air with ease, which made him a great pass receiver. His own passing was almost perfect. His shot, while not strong, was incredibly accurate.

# SPORTS STAR ★ WAYNE GRETZKY

But the main thing some scouts saw in Wayne was his amazing ability to anticipate what was going to happen next in a game where everything happens so quickly. He was always one step ahead of the other players. He knew what everyone was doing and would do. He was a kind of chess player on ice.

There is some medical evidence that great athletes can see action in a kind of slow motion, so they have more time to plan their moves. Wayne says that he has made as much of a study of hockey as doctors do of learning about their profession, so he knows every possible play. Whatever it is, Wayne has an incredible ability to be at the right place at the right time.

At the time Wayne was coming along, professional hockey was expanding, and the leagues were looking around for young players to fill up their teams. On Sunday, July 11, 1978, aboard the owner's private jet, Wayne signed a four-year contract worth $875,000 with the Indianapolis Racers of the World Hockey League.

"Before I signed that contract," Wayne said, "the most money I ever had of my own was $260." He was just seventeen.

SPORTS STAR   WAYNE GRETZKY

Despite the fact that he was now earning a big salary, Wayne still lived with a family instead of getting his own apartment. He went to night school to take twelfth grade courses. He had promised his parents that he would finish high school.

Wayne played only eight games with the Racers before financial problems forced the owner to sell Wayne's contract. Sports fans in Indianapolis seem to like watching cars go around better than looking at the strange game of ice hockey.

Peter Pocklington, the owner of the Edmonton Oilers of the World Hockey League, bought the Gretzky contract. He signed Wayne up for nine years with two six-year options. Wayne agreed to play for the Oilers for the next twenty-one years. His salary was to be about $300,000 a year.

In January, 1979, on Wayne's eighteenth birthday, Pocklington held a ceremony at the center of the ice rink. With a baby-sized bottle of champagne and a birthday cake in the shape of a 99 (Wayne's number since his Sault Ste. Marie days), he told the world he had signed Gretzky to a twenty-one-year

As Wayne's father, Walter Gretzky, and Larry Gordon, the former General Manager of the Oilers, look on, Wayne signs his contract with the Edmonton Oilers. Two of his three younger brothers can be seen behind their father.

contract. It was the longest contract in the history of professional sports.

Wayne went to work to earn his money. In professional hockey a player scores a goal whenever he puts the puck into the net by himself. He gets credit for an assist whenever he makes a pass that leads to a goal. He earns a point for each goal and each assist that he makes. Wayne finished his WHA season with 46 goals and 64 assists, which added up to a total of 110 points.

Just as important as his scoring record was the fact that Wayne did not miss a game. He proved he could handle the faster pace and bigger players of the pro game.

During his first year in Edmonton, Wayne finally got his high school diploma by taking courses at the Ross Sheppard Composite

High School. He did much of his homework on buses, trains, and airplanes.

In strength tests that the Oilers gave their players in 1979, Wayne Gretzky finished last. He joked with the doctors by asking them if he was stronger than his mother. But on tests that measured endurance and recuperative powers, Wayne performed exceptionally well.

# SPORTS STAR — WAYNE GRETZKY

Just before the 1979–80 hockey season started, the World Hockey Association and the National Hockey League merged. Sports reporters wrote they were sure the skinny eighteen-year-old who had torn up the WHA would not put on much of a show in the stronger NHL.

That was all Gretzky needed to hear. He had always enjoyed proving his critics wrong. He set a goal for himself. He was determined to get as many points in his first year in the NHL as he had in his WHA season. Wayne did so well that he probably surprised even himself. He tied for the league scoring championship with 137 points. He won the Lady Byng Memorial Trophy as the NHL's most gentlemanly player, and he was named the league's Most Valuable Player.

Peter Pocklington, owner of the Edmonton Oilers

Walter Gretzky had always told his son to concentrate first of all on getting what he wanted most and the other good things like fame and money would follow. When the 1979-80 season was completed, Peter Pocklington gave Wayne an expensive, sporty Ferrari car. His father's advice was beginning to pay off.

★ SPORTS STAR ★ WAYNE GRETZKY ★

Meanwhile, Walter Gretzky was busy turning his other sons into champion hockey players. Thirteen-year-old Keith began to break his brother's peewee records. Eight-year-old Brent was playing with older boys and beginning to be a big scorer.

Glen Gretzky was born with a club foot. He did not begin skating until he was six. After three operations a pin was put in his foot. He had trouble skating and making turns, but he was determined to master the sport. When the other kids went inside because it was too cold, Glen stayed outside to practice. When Glen made a local all-star team, his parents were as proud of him as they had ever been of Wayne or any of their other children.

SPORTS STAR  WAYNE GRETZKY

# 4
# A TEAM GROWS UP

All those who watched the Edmonton Oilers as they began their second season in the NHL could not help but notice how young the players looked. As a matter of fact, they were the youngest team in NHL history. Three of the best players, including Wayne, were only nineteen years old. Most of the others were in their early twenties. They looked more like eager college students than professional hockey players.

Edmonton, Alberta

# SPORTS STAR ★ WAYNE GRETZKY

Edmonton is a town that is growing fast as a result of oil located under the vast Alberta prairie. A person has to be fairly rugged to live there. In the middle of winter, the temperatures range from minus 15 to minus 35 degrees Centigrade. That's plus 5 to minus 31 degrees Fahrenheit. Therefore, the people who have been attracted to Edmonton are, for the most part, young, enthusiastic, and sure of themselves.

When Edmonton joined the NHL, Manager Glen Sather built his team on speed and youth rather than on experience.

Through most of the team's first two years in the NHL, the Oilers did not behave like champions. At the beginning of the 1980-81 season, they played so badly that a coaching change was made. Manager Glen Sather also took on the job of coach.

Glen Sather, general manager and coach of the Edmonton Oilers

Still the team was unpredictable. The Oilers often defeated teams that no one expected them to beat, and then they would turn around and lose to teams they should have defeated.

Only the top sixteen of the twenty-one NHL teams are invited to play in the Stanley Cup play-offs. For most of the season the

SPORTS STAR  WAYNE GRETZKY

struggling Oilers, even with a super star like Wayne Gretzky on their team, were at the bottom of the hockey standings. It didn't look as if they would make the play-offs.

All of a sudden, when there was only one month left in the regular season, a miracle seemed to take place. Almost overnight all the young stars began to work together. The Oilers made a remarkable surge and lost only four of their final twenty games.

Their youth and enthusiasm caught the attention of hockey fans throughout the league. They were a breath of fresh air in a sport that was beginning to be dominated by some players who won by violence and not skill.

The Oilers were a bunch of kids who could skate incredibly fast, passed often, used intricate plays, and frequently skated circles around the older players. The team reminded many fans of their own youth. As they had grown up and played hockey on lakes and rivers during the cold Canadian winters, they found the game rough, but it was one that involved mostly skating skills.

Professional hockey
is not always fun.

# SPORTS STAR ★ WAYNE GRETZKY

All season long it was Number 99, Wayne Gretzky, who was the heart of the team. He failed to score a point in only sixteen of the eighty games the Oilers played, and the Oilers lost every game in which Gretzky was shut out. Wayne set a record by taking part in exactly half of Edmonton's goals. He gave his teammates many chances to make goals by setting them up to score. As a result, every man on the team wanted to play on Wayne's line. Gretzky was and always has been very much a team player.

At the end of his second NHL season, Wayne's total of 164 points broke Phil Esposito's single-season scoring record. His 109 assists broke the assist record set by Bobby Orr. Both records had stood for ten years and had never been seriously threatened. In addition, Wayne became the

Wayne poses with his trophies, the Hart trophy for the NHL Most Valuable Player and the Art Ross trophy for the most points gained during the regular season.

first NHL player since 1917-18 to average more than two points a game, and he won his second Most Valuable Player Award.

The Oilers finished the regular season in a very unimpressive fourteenth place, but it was good enough to put them into the

SPORTS STAR ★ WAYNE GRETZKY

Stanley Cup play-offs. In the first round they had to meet the mighty Montreal Canadiens, who had won the Stanley Cup more often than any other team.

For years the Canadiens' Guy Lafleur had been the leading Canadian hockey player. Montreal fans did not think the kids from Edmonton stood much of a chance against their experienced team.

Before the first game in the three-out-of-five series, the Canadien goaltender, Richard Sevigny, went so far as to say that Lafleur would put Gretzky in his back pocket. Sevigny should probably have kept quiet.

Wayne Gretzky led his team to one of the most remarkable opening-game upsets in the history of the Stanley Cup. He did it by not taking a single shot on goal himself.

Instead, he passed to his teammates and got credit for a record-setting five assists. The Oilers won 6–3. After the sixth goal, Gretzky skated by Richard Sevigny in front of the Canadien net and smugly patted his back pocket.

When Edmonton won the second game, the Montreal fans rose to applaud the Oilers as they celebrated their victory at center ice.

SPORTS STAR  WAYNE GRETZKY

It was as if the fans knew the hockey leadership was passing from Ron Lafleur to Wayne Gretzky. It was a sad thing for Montreal fans, but it could not be ignored.

Before the third game the Oilers' manager and coach, Glen Sather, played for his team tapes of the first two games, along with a recording of the song, "The Impossible Dream." The young Oilers were so excited that nothing could stop them. The Montreal fans gave the Oilers a standing ovation when the team skated onto the ice for the third game.

Wayne Gretzky scored three goals in the final game, which the Oilers won 6-2. It was the first time since 1952 that Montreal had been eliminated from the Stanley Cup competition without a single victory. It was the most incredible play-off upset anyone could remember. The Oilers had become a national phenomenon.

In the next round the Oilers lost to the defending Stanley Cup champion New York Islanders four games to two. Still the series was closer than New York ever dreamed it would be. The Oilers had proved that they could be the team to beat in the near future.

Wayne about to score in
the play-offs against Montreal

 SPORTS STAR  WAYNE GRETZKY

# 5

# THE 1981-82 SEASON

The Edmonton Oilers began the 1981-1982 season where they had left off—by winning again and again. "We went through bad times together, grew up together," said Wayne. "Now's our time to win together."

The Oilers became the slickest, quickest, most explosive club in the NHL, and the fans loved them. They outscored every other hockey team in their division and easily stayed in first place all season long.

Wayne Gretzky often lets out a whoop of pleasure and kicks one leg in the air after scoring a goal.

SPORTS STAR ★ WAYNE GRETZKY

A lot of the credit for their success, of course, had to go to Wayne Gretzky, who hard as it might be to believe, kept getting better all the time. But the Oilers were not a one-man team. At least six of the other players were good enough to be on the NHL All-Star team. The Oilers' Grant Fuhr, the first and only black goaltender in the NHL, had the best goalie percentage in the league at the end of 1981–82 season.

For Wayne Gretzky, the 1981–82 season was one in which he would shatter almost every single-season scoring record in the NHL record book. One of the best known was the 50-goals-in-50-games record held jointly by Maurice Richard of the Montreal Canadiens and Mike Bossy of the New York Islanders. By late fall it was fairly clear that Wayne would break that record, but it happened sooner than anyone expected.

On the night of January 30 the Oilers were playing the Philadelphia Flyers in Edmonton. It was the thirty-ninth game of the season. Going into the game, Wayne had 45 goals.

Seven minutes into the first period Gretzky was parked at the edge of the Flyers' net when he flicked a rebound from teammate Paul Coffey past goaltender Pete Peeters to tie the score at 1-1.

Those who know him best say that there are times when Wayne Gretzky's blue eyes light up in a way that says, "Tonight, tonight." After that first goal, Oiler teammate Ron Low, sitting on the bench, was the only one to notice that special gleam in Gretzky's eyes. Low said to Coach Sather, "Betcha he'll do it tonight."

SPORTS STAR  WAYNE GRETZKY

Less than three minutes later Gretzky picked up goal number 47 with a 20-foot slapshot under the crossbar. The slapshot is the most powerful shot in hockey. A player wishing to use it swings back his stick and wallops the puck as hard as possible. Three minutes into the second period, Wayne completed the hat trick (three goals in one game) with a 25-foot slapshot over Peeters' right shoulder.

Gretzky's fourth goal of the game came five minutes into the final period, when he grabbed the puck at the blue line, swept around defenseman Bob Hoffmeyer, and sent a 20-foot drive over the netminder's gloved hand. The climax of that memorable evening came with only three seconds left in the game. Taking a pass from teammate Glenn Anderson, Wayne fired a shot from

As Number 50 rolls into the net, Wayne cheers along with thousands of his fans.

the Philadelphia blue line into the vacant net for goal number 50.

Gretzky was immediately buried as his teammates rushed to congratulate him. The cheers of 17,490 fans rang in his ears. Even after the game ended, the clapping and yelling went on.

For Wayne, however, the pressure did not seem to let up. As soon as he broke the 50-goals-in-50-games record, both fans and reporters began the countdown for breaking Phil Esposito's record of 76 goals scored in a single season, set in 1971.

As Wayne neared the breaking of that record, Phil Esposito began following the Oilers from city to city in order to be on hand when the historic moment took place. Wayne scored the record-breaking goal (number 77) in Buffalo with sixteen games still left to play.

When Wayne Gretzky finished his third season in the NHL in early April, he had 92 goals. He had surpassed Phil Esposito's record by an amazing sixteen goals!

Wayne also broke his own records. He had 120 assists, which were eleven more

Phil Esposito and Wayne Gretzky at a press conference after Wayne scored a goal to tie Esposito's record of 76 goals in a single season.

than he had in the previous year. He had 212 points, which were 48 more than he had in the 1980–81 season.

That was not all. Gretzky set an NHL record for the most three-goal games. He had ten of them, including one five-goal game and three four-goal games.

The Oilers also had a sensational season. They easily won the championship of the Smythe Division. The New York Islanders were the only team ahead of them in the overall National Hockey League standings.

# SPORTS STAR ★ WAYNE GRETZKY

This time there was no question about the Oilers being in the Stanley Cup play-offs, and they were regarded as having a good chance of winning the championship. The Edmonton Oilers faced the Los Angeles Kings in the first round. The first two games were played in Edmonton.

The year before the little-known Oilers had upset mighty Montreal in the opening round. This year it was the Oilers who were toppled by a team with a poor regular season record.

The Los Angeles Kings surprised the Edmonton fans by winning the first game of the three-out-of-five series. Then with the score tied at 2-2 at the end of the second game, Wayne Gretzky scored during overtime with a 45-foot slapshot to lead the Oilers to a 3-2 victory.

With the series tied at one game apiece, the two teams flew to Los Angeles for games three and four. In the third game the Oilers blew a 5-0 third-period lead and lost by a score of 6-5. After the game the Edmonton dressing room was closed to reporters for twenty minutes.

Later Wayne told newsmen, "All year long we've been such an explosive hockey team. Now I don't know what to say. We didn't play hard all three periods. Now we'd better do it all three periods Monday night."

Unfortunately, the Oilers could not get back the magic that had worked for them all year long. On Monday, April 12, they were knocked out of the play-offs when they lost to the Kings by a score of 3-2.

It had to have been a big disappointment to Wayne and his teammates to lose so

SPORTS STAR  WAYNE GRETZKY

early in Stanley Cup play. Still, they were very pleased with the way they played all season long.

Wayne Gretzky had every reason to be proud of himself. At twenty-one years of age, in only his third season in the National Hockey League, he had played better and broken more records than any offensive player in the long history of professional hockey.

Ice hockey, especially in Canada, has created some heroes known to every kid who shoves a puck around a rink. Howie Morenz, Maurice Richard, Gordie Howe, Bobby Hull, and Bobby Orr are men whose genius on the ice turned them into legends. Wayne Gretzky is likely to become a legend in his twenties and may well be the greatest of them all.

A familiar sight—Wayne Gretzky scoring. (Wayne is playing for Team Canada in this picture.)

# PLAYING RECORD

## WAYNE GRETZKY

| SEASON | CLUB | LEAGUE | REGULAR SCHEDULE ||||| PLAY-OFFS |||||
|---|---|---|---|---|---|---|---|---|---|---|---|---|
| | | | GAMES PLAYED | GOALS | ASSISTS | TOTAL POINTS | PENALTIES IN MINUTES | GAMES PLAYED | GOALS | ASSISTS | TOTAL POINTS | PENALTIES IN MINUTES |
| 1978-79 | Indianapolis | WHA | 8 | 3 | 3 | 6 | 0 | - | - | - | - | - |
| 1978-79 | Edmonton | WHA | 72 | 43 | 61 | 104 | 19 | 13 | *10 | 10 | *20 | 2 |
| 1979-80 | Edmonton | NHL | 79 | 51 | 86 | 137 | 21 | 3 | 2 | 1 | 3 | 0 |
| 1980-81 | Edmonton | NHL | 80 | 55 | *109 | *164 | 28 | 9 | 7 | 14 | 21 | 4 |
| 1981-82 | Edmonton | NHL | 80 | *92 | *120 | *212 | 26 | 5 | 5 | 7 | 12 | 8 |
| | WHA Totals | | 80 | 46 | 64 | 110 | 19 | 13 | 10 | 10 | 20 | 2 |
| | NHL Totals | | 239 | 198 | 315 | 513 | 75 | 17 | 14 | 22 | 36 | 12 |

*Establishes new record